ENVIRONMENTAL ACTION
Analyze **C**onsider options **T**ake action **I**n **O**ur **N**eighborhoods

WATER
Conservation

A Student Audit of Resource Use

STUDENT EDITION

E2: ENVIRONMENT & EDUCATION

DALE SEYMOUR PUBLICATIONS®

Developed by E2: Environment & Education™, an activity of the Tides Center.

Managing Editor: Cathy Anderson
Senior Editor: Jeri Hayes
Production/Manufacturing Director: Janet Yearian
Design Manager: Jeff Kelly
Senior Production Coordinator: Alan Noyes
Text and Cover Design: Lynda Banks Design
Art: Rachel Gage
Composition: Andrea Reider
Clip Art Illustrations: Copyright © Art Parts, Courtesy Art Parts, 714-834-9166

Copyright © 1998 by The Tides Center/E2: Environment & Education. Published by Dale Seymour Publications®, an imprint of Pearson Learning Group, 299 Jefferson Road, Parsippany, NJ 07054. All rights reserved. No part of this book may be reproduced or transmitted in any form or by any means, electronic, or mechanical, including photocopying, recording, or by any information storage and retrieval system, without permission in writing from the publisher. For information regarding permission(s), write to Rights and Permissions Department.

Printed on Acid-Free, 85% recycled paper (15% post-consumer), using soy-based ink.

ISBN 0-201-49539-2
Printed in the United States of America
3 4 5 6 7 8 9   06 05 04 03 02

1-800-321-3106
www.pearsonlearning.com

CONTENTS

Welcome to Environmental ACTION!

EXPLORE the Issues

1 EXPLORE Identify Water as a Limited Resource — 9
  Activity Sheet 1: The Water Cycle — 11

2 EXPLORE Evaluate World and U.S. Water Use — 12
  Activity Sheet 2: World Water Use Graph — 15

3 EXPLORE Identify Sources and Effects of Water Pollution — 16
  Activity Sheet 3: Sources of Water Pollution — 19

4 EXPLORE Practice Water Conservation — 20
  Activity Sheet 4: Conserving Water — 23

ANALYZE

5 ANALYZE Learn About Community Water Resources — 27
  Activity Sheet 5: Notes On Your Community Water Supply — 29

6 ANALYZE Learn About Your School Water System — 30
  Activity Sheet 6: School Water System — 32

7 ANALYZE Plan Your Water Audit — 33
  Activity Sheet 7: Water Audit Plan — 35

Contents v

8 ANALYZE	Begin Your Water Audit	36
	Activity Sheet 8: Action Group Plan	38
9 ANALYZE	Complete Your Water Audit	39
	Activity Sheet 9: Water Use Chart	41
10 ANALYZE	Read a Water Meter and Water Bill	42
	Activity Sheet 10: Read a Water Bill	45
11 ANALYZE	Summarize Findings	46
	Activity Sheet 11: School Water Use Chart	48

Act Locally 49

CONSIDER OPTIONS

12 CONSIDER OPTIONS	Brainstorm Water Conservation Ideas	53
	Activity Sheet 12: Brainstorm Solutions	55
13 CONSIDER OPTIONS	Weigh the Costs and Benefits	56
	Activity Sheet 13: Assessing Costs and Benefits	58
14 CONSIDER OPTIONS	Make Conservation Recommendations	59
	Activity Sheet 14: Water Conservation Proposal	61

Act Locally 62

TAKE ACTION

Choose Conservation Measures		65
Activity Sheet 15: Rating Sheet		67
Prepare and Present Proposal		68
Activity Sheet 16: Proposal Checklist		70
Track Response to Proposal		71
Activity Sheet 17: Tracking Sheet		73

Appendices

Issues and Information

Section A	Water on Earth	77
Section B	Uses of Water	82
Section C	Water Pollution and Treatment	85
Section D	Water Conservation Technology and Practices	90
Section E	Water Meters and Water Bills	96
Section F	Measuring Water	99
Glossary		100

Welcome to Environmental ACTION!

Welcome to Environmental ACTION!

This environmental program is designed to give you the knowledge and tools you need to make choices that will make a real difference to your quality of life, both now and in your future. You and all other living things modify the environment in order to live. What are the consequences of your actions on the food supply, atmosphere, and water cycle? The interrelationships of living things and long-term effects of actions are only beginning to be understood. As human beings, we are unique among Earth's organisms because we can choose to change our daily behavior. We can change our actions to reduce our impact on the environment, improve our quality of life, and provide for the needs of future generations. We can conserve and preserve our natural resources.

Using your school as a laboratory, you will investigate environmental issues and analyze how they influence human health and the environment. Each module contains a set of ACT activities that will guide you in your investigations. ACT stands for

- Analyze
- Consider Options
- Take Action

When you have completed your investigation and compiled your research, you will present a proposal for change to your school environmental committee.

What features does a lifestyle with a sustainable future have?

It is renewable. Resources are replaced as they are used.
It is balanced. People and systems work together to improve the environment in the present and to ensure the quality of life in the future.
It is manageable. Products are reusable, recyclable, and biodegradable.

Your Journal

Throughout the project, you will be using a Journal. It is a notebook in which you record all your observations and data, write down ideas, make sketches, and outline procedures.

You will need to use your Journal when you are conducting research in a study area, so it should be easy to carry. Your teacher may have specific instructions on what kind of notebook to use.

Action Groups

For most of the activities in this program, you spend part of your time working in a group. Your Action Group will work cooperatively, so that the group members benefit from each other's contributions. Sharing ideas, determining the best steps to take to achieve a goal, and dividing up tasks are just some of the advantages of working together.

Home activities can be done individually, but you may find that you prefer working with a group. Try to include your parents, brothers and sisters, or other family members in your work at home.

Topic Descriptions

The Environmental ACTION project that you are about to begin is one of six modules, or units. Each module focuses on a different aspect of the environment. Your teacher may choose to do only one module, a few modules, or all of the modules. The modules cover the following topics:

Energy Conservation

Using the school as a research laboratory, you'll explore where energy comes from and how it is used, the effect of energy production on the environment, and how to improve energy efficiency at school and at home.

Food Choices

You will investigate the effects of food production, diet, and nutrition on human health and the environment. You will analyze your school's food service programs and identify healthy choices and practices.

Habitat and Biodiversity

You will study the importance of biological diversity, landscape management, xeriscaping, composting, and integrated pest management (IPM). You'll tour the school grounds to assess the current landscaping lay-out and then evaluate the present condition in relation to environmental sustainability. This module also contains a step-by-step guide on how to create an organic garden and a seed bank.

Chemicals: Choosing Wisely

You will investigate the use of hazardous materials—paints, chemical products, cleaning supplies, pesticides—how they are stored and disposed of, and their potential effects on human health and the environment. After evaluating the results, you develop a plan for implementing the use of Earth- and human-friendly alternatives at school and home.

Waste Reduction

After you sort your school's garbage to identify recyclable and compostable materials and analyze the school's current waste practices, you will formulate a plan to reduce your consumption and waste at school and at home. Development or improvement of a recycling program may be part of the process.

Water Conservation

After an introduction to water consumption and water-quality issues, you'll conduct an audit of water usage and efficiency to determine whether current consumption practices on campus can be improved. You will then develop strategies for implementing water conservation at school and home.

Explore the Issues

IDENTIFY WATER AS A LIMITED RESOURCE

Seen as a blue orb from space, Earth is often called the "water planet." Water covers three-fourths of the earth and is essential to all life. However, only a small portion of Earth's water is available for human use. All water passes through a continuous cycle. Find out about the water cycle to better understand this limited resource.

Setting the Stage

Discuss these questions:
1. Where does the water you use come from?
2. What might limit the supply of water available for you to use?

Vocabulary

- evaporation
- groundwater
- precipitation
- respiration
- transpiration

Focus

A. Imagine that the gallon container of water in the diagram below represents all the water on Earth. Study the diagram and then discuss the questions. Additional material about water on the earth can be found in Issues and Information section A.

THINK ABOUT IT

"Water, water, everywhere,

Nor any drop to drink."

—Samuel Coleridge, "The Rime of the Ancient Mariner," Part II Stanza 9

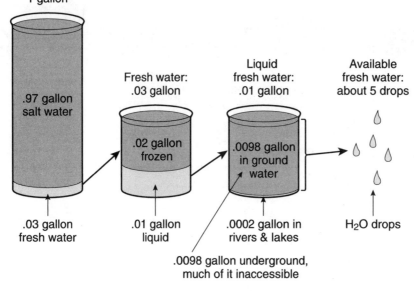

1. What percentage of water on Earth is salt water?
2. What portion of fresh water on Earth is frozen in glaciers and ice caps?
3. What are the sources of drinking water?
4. What are some problems in taking water from groundwater sources?

B. Complete all the work on Activity Sheet 1. Refer to Issues and Information section A for a full description of the water cycle.

It's a Wrap

On a separate sheet of paper, write a sentence or short paragraph to answer the following questions.

1. Why is it said that our view of how much water is available is an "illusion of plenty"?
2. What are some possible ways to protect the amount of available fresh water?

Home

In your Journal, list all the activities you do that depend on water. Keep this record from the moment you leave the classroom until you get back to it the next day (or until 24 hours have passed).

Your teacher will give you a two-part activity sheet like the one below to use with this lesson.

ACTIVITY SHEET

Name

THE WATER CYCLE (part 1)

Complete this drawing of the water cycle. Draw arrows and label the pathways of evaporation, respiration, transpiration, and precipitation. Then answer the questions below.

1. The amount of water on the earth is the same as it ever was or ever will be. How can this statement be true if we are using water all the time?

Explore the Issues: Identify Water as a Limited Resource

EVALUATE WORLD AND U.S. WATER USE

We depend on water for countless purposes: we drink it and use it in our food, we grow our crops with it, we make products with it, we use it for recreation and to create pleasing environments. Find out about our increasing use of water and how water use differs throughout the world.

Setting the Stage

Discuss these questions:
1. What do you use water for?
2. Why might people use different amounts of water?

Vocabulary

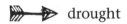 drought

Focus

A. Study the graph and then discuss the questions. Additional material about water use can be found in Issues and Information section B.
   1. How much greater was world water use in 1950 than in 1900? Two times greater? Three times greater?
   2. How much greater is world water use predicted to be in 2000 than it was in 1900? Will it be two times greater? Five times greater? Ten times greater?
   3. For what purpose is most water in the world used? What is the second biggest use of water? What is the third biggest use of water?

> **THINK ABOUT IT**
>
> "In the mountains of Nepal, women may... climb 1000 meters down steep slopes to a river and then carry water back up, sometimes twice a day."
>
> *Women of the World: The Facts*, "Women and Water," by OUTREACH (Source: Women, Health, and Development, Development Education Centre, UNICEF, Palais des Nations, CH-1211 Geneva 10, Switzerland

12   Environmental ACTION   Water

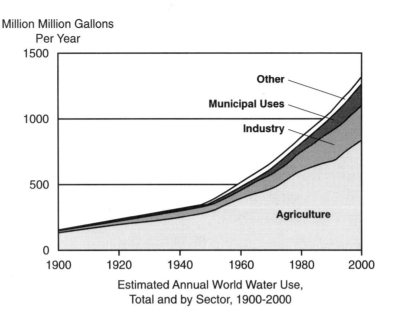

Estimated Annual World Water Use,
Total and by Sector, 1900-2000

4. World population doubled between 1950 and 1990. Is it correct to say that the increase in world water use in those years can be completely explained by the increase in population? Why or why not?

B. Study this chart about how much water is used in the U.S. for different purposes and discuss the questions.

Producing Agricultural Products		Producing Industrial Products	
Water Required	**To Produce One Pound of**	**Water Required**	**To Produce**
24 gallons	potatoes	25 gallons	1 gallon of gasoline
33 gallons	carrots	35 gallons	1 pound of steel
65 gallons	oranges	80 gallons	1 Sunday newspaper
560 gallons	rice	1000 gallons	1 pound of aluminum
815 gallons	chicken	82,000 gallons	1 ton of brown paper for bags
2607 gallons	beef	100,000 gallons	1 automobile

Explore the Issues: Evaluate World and U.S. Water Use

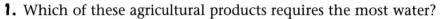

1. Which of these agricultural products requires the most water?
2. How do you think the water is used to produce this product?
3. Which of these industrial products requires the most water?
4. Complete all the work on Activity Sheet 2.

It's a Wrap

On a separate sheet of paper, answer the following questions.

1. Why has water use increased so dramatically in the last century?
2. What are the biggest uses of water worldwide?
3. How could you or your community cut down on water use if water were scarce, such as during a drought? Name three ways.

Home

In your Journal, look at the list you made in Activity 1. Imagine that you had only a limited amount of water to use in a day. Which water-using activities could you eliminate? Which are essential? Prioritize your list by writing "high priority," "medium priority," or "low priority" beside each entry.

Your teacher will give you a two-part activity sheet like the one below to use with this lesson.

ACTIVITY SHEET

Name

WORLD WATER USE GRAPH (part 1)

Rank the countries in the chart below by the amount of water used in a day. Then display the information in a bar graph.

1990 Water Use Per Person
(Including agricultural and industrial use)

Country	Gallons Per Day	Rank by Water Use
Australia	945	
Canada	1268	
China	334	
Colombia	129	
Kenya	35	
Germany	466	
Japan	668	
United States	1565	

Gallons Per Day

1600
1400
1200
1000
800
600
400
200
0

Countries

IDENTIFY SOURCES AND EFFECTS OF WATER POLLUTION

One of our most serious environmental problems is pollution in surface and groundwater. The pollutants include toxic chemicals, oils, metals, and bacteria. Although legislation in the U.S. has helped to reduce contamination, widespread sources of pollution continue to increase and are difficult to control.

Setting the Stage

Discuss these questions:
1. What does polluted water look like?
2. What are some sources of water pollution in the U.S.?
3. What are some of the environmental and health effects of water pollution?

Vocabulary

> deforestation
> landfills
> nonpoint-source pollution
> nutrients
> point-source pollution
> runoff
> septic systems
> toxins

Focus

A. Study the chart and then discuss the questions. Additional material on water pollution can be found in Issues and Information section C.

THINK ABOUT IT

"Millions of pounds of toxic chemicals, like lead, mercury and pesticides, pour into our waterways each year, contaminating wildlife, seafood and drinking water. One-half of our nation's lakes and one-third of our rivers are too polluted to be completely safe for swimming or fishing."

Natural Resources Defense Council, *25 Year Report*, 1995, p. 10

16 Environmental ACTION Water

	Some Common Water Pollutants				
	Bacteria	Nutrients	Ammonia	Acids	Toxins
City sewage treatment plants	X	X	X		X
Industrial facilities				X	X
Sewer overflows	X	X	X		X
Agricultural runoff	X	X			X
Urban runoff	X	X			X
Construction runoff		X			X
Mining runoff				X	X
Septic systems	X	X			X
Landfill sites					X
Forestry runoff		X			X

1. Which pollutants can come from many different sources?
2. How do nutrients act as water pollutants?
3. What are some sources of the bacteria and toxins in agricultural runoff?
4. What are some sources of the toxins in urban runoff and landfill sites?

B. Complete all the work on Activity Sheet 3. Refer to Issues and Information sections C and D to help you complete the activity.

It's a Wrap

Choose one source of water pollution and develop a plan or design to educate people about it and suggest ways to reduce it. You might make a poster, write a radio ad, or create a design or slogan to paint on storm drains. You may wish to refer to materials in Issues and Information sections C and D.

Home

In your Journal, make a list of activities you have observed at home, at school, or in your community that might be contributing to water pollution.

Your teacher will give you a two-part activity sheet like the one below to use with this lesson.

Explore the Issues: Identify Sources and Effects of Water Pollution   19

PRACTICE WATER CONSERVATION

Water conservation is essential so that enough fresh water is available to meet our present and future needs. Conserving fresh water means both using less water and reducing water pollution. Find out about the importance of water conservation and how to practice it.

Setting the Stage

Discuss these questions:
1. What are some indications that water conservation is needed?
2. How can you practice water conservation in your daily life?

Vocabulary

➤ aerator
biodegradable
phosphate

THINK ABOUT IT

"The average car wash uses 40 gallons of water for each car. Each year in the United States about 160 million gallons of water are used to wash cars."

"Water: The Source of Life," from the *1992 The Year of Clean Water Calendar*, America's Clean Water Foundation, 1992, p. 17

Focus

A. Study the pictures and captions on page 21, and then discuss the questions. Refer to Issues and Information section D for more about water conservation technologies and practices.
   1. How can you conserve water when you are at home?
   2. How can you conserve water at school?
   3. Name some ways to conserve water that are not shown in the pictures.
B. Complete all the work on Activity Sheet 4.

20 Environmental ACTION Water

Don't leave water running.

Install water-saving showerheads.

Plant plants that do not need much water.

Repair leaky faucets.

Use biodegradable products that do not contain phosphates.

Dispose of chemicals properly.

Don't put trash in streams or lakes.

Use fewer herbicides and fertilizers.

It's a Wrap

On a separate sheet of paper, write a sentence or short paragraph to answer the following questions.

1. What are the two general categories of water-conserving measures?

2. Water is very cheap in the U.S. (the average price is $1.30 for 1000 gallons). Do you think it would be better if people had to pay more for water? Explain your ideas.

3. What are some ways to encourage people to practice water conservation?

Home

In your Journal, make the following chart.

Water-Using or Polluting Activities	Ways to Conserve Water

In the first column, list at least three of your water-using activities from the Home assignment in Activity 1 and at least three of the water-polluting activities from the Home assignment in Activity 3. In the second column, list ways to reduce the amount of water used or the pollutants added to water for each activity.

Your teacher will give you an activity sheet like the one below to use with this lesson.

ACTIVITY SHEET 4 EXPLORE

Name

CONSERVING WATER

In the U.S. each day we use more than 5 billion gallons of fresh water to flush toilets and more than 3 billion gallons to shower. Get an idea of how much water can be saved by replacing old fixtures with new, water-efficient models. Read the information, then complete the chart below.

- Standard faucets use as much as 7 gallons of water per minute. A faucet with a simple water-saving aerator uses as little as 4.2 gallons per minute.
- Standard shower heads use 5 or more gallons of water per minute. A low-flow shower head uses about 1.5 gallons per minute.
- Common toilets use about 7 gallons per flush. Some of the new low-flush toilets use as little as 1.6 gallons per flush.
- The average price of water in the U.S. is .0013 cents per gallon.

	Standard	Water-Efficient	Savings for One Use	Savings for 1000 Uses
Faucets				
Gallons of Water Used*				
Cost				
Shower Heads				
Gallons of Water Used*				
Cost				
Toilets				
Gallons of Water Used				
Cost				

* Assume 5-minute faucet use and 5-minute shower.

Analyze

LEARN ABOUT COMMUNITY WATER RESOURCES

In this activity, you will learn about your community's water supply from a local expert. The resource person will speak to you about where your community's water supply comes from, how plentiful it is, measures taken to protect it, and other issues affecting water resources in your community.

Setting the Stage

Discuss these questions:
1. What is the biggest problem affecting your community's water supply?
2. What is your community water utility doing to ensure an adequate water supply for the future?

Focus

A. Before the speaker visits, work with one or two classmates to brainstorm questions you would like answered about your community's water supply. Prepare written questions so that you will be sure to obtain complete, detailed information. Use the ideas below to help fuel your brainstorming:

1. Where does the community water supply come from? Are there other possible water sources?
2. Is the water source polluted? Where does the pollution come from?
3. How is the community water supply treated to make it safe for use? How is it tested? How often? What pollutants is it tested for?
4. How is water used in the community? Is it primarily used in households or does much of it go to industry or agriculture? What kind of industry or agriculture? How does the usage change from season to season?

> **THINK ABOUT IT**
>
> "The rivers and lakes sustain us; they flow through the veins of the earth and into our own. But we must take care to let them flow back out as pure as they came, not poison and waste them without thought for the future."
>
> Senator Al Gore, *Earth in the Balance*, Houghton Mifflin Co., 1992, p. 114

Analyze: Learn About Community Water Resources

5. How is the way people are using water changing? Are changes in population affecting the need for water? Will the community need more water in the future?
6. How important is water conservation to the community water supply? What conservation measures does the community take?

B. Use Activity Sheet 5 to record information you learn from the resource person. This information will be helpful as you proceed with the activities in this program.

It's a Wrap

Discuss the information you collected on Activity Sheet 5. Feel free to change or add information to your chart.

Using what you have learned, discuss the questions you explored earlier: What is the biggest problem affecting the community water supply? How is water being conserved in your community? What plans are being made to meet water needs in the future?

Home

Interview members of your family to find out what they know about the water supply. What are the primary uses of water in your household? What is the biggest single use? Does the cost of water affect how your family uses this resource? Has your family tried to reduce water consumption? How? Use your Journal to record family members' responses.

Your teacher will give you a two-part activity sheet like the one below to use with this lesson.

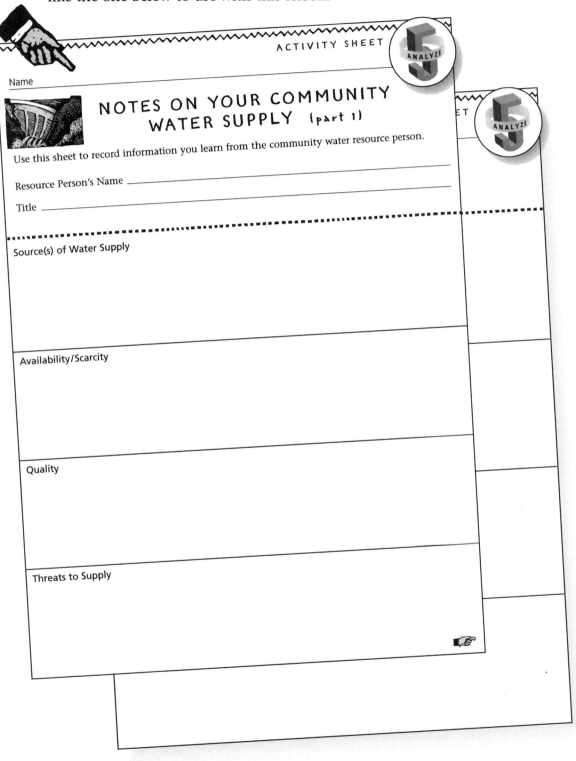

Analyze: Learn About Community Water Resources

LEARN ABOUT YOUR SCHOOL WATER SYSTEM

Learn how water is used in your school. An expert on your school's water system will guide you on a tour of your school and explain current water uses, conservation measures, and how the system works. Be alert to all the places and ways in which water is used.

Setting the Stage

Discuss these questions:
1. How is water used in your school?
2. What are some of the different water use areas in your school?
3. Does your school practice water conservation? Why? How is water conserved?

Focus

A. Your school's water system serves the entire campus. As you tour the campus, notice the location of the water meter and where the school system connects to the community system. Observe all water outlets, meters, equipment, and other fixtures. Pay attention to the different ways in which water is used. Note the location of drinking fountains, faucets, rest rooms, showers, sinks, sprinklers. Look for places where water is used for special purposes, such as the kitchen, swimming pool, and locker room. Find out whether any of these areas has special water use equipment, such as automatic dish washers. The following questions can be used to help you gather information.

1. What are some ways the school attempts to conserve water? Have water-saving fixtures been installed?

> **THINK ABOUT IT**
> People can exist on a gallon or so of water a day.... In medieval times people probably used no more than three to five gallons a day. In the 19th century...we began using about 95 gallons a day. At present in the United States, an individual uses about 1500 gallons of water a day for... [basic needs], recreation, cooling, food production, and industrial supply.
>
> —Jack E. Gartrell, Jr.; Jane Crowder; Jeffrey C. Callister, *Earth: The Water Planet,* p. 159 (from "Conservation and the Water Cycle," United States Department of Agriculture, Soil Conservation Service, Agriculture Information Bulletin No. 326

2. Are there special systems, such as an irrigation system for the athletic field or a sprinkler system for fire protection?
3. How frequently and for how long are the athletic fields, lawns, and garden areas watered?
4. What water applications use the most water?

B. Use Activity Sheet 6 and your Journal to record what you find out during your tour.

It's a Wrap

Review your work on Activity Sheet 6. What did you find out about how water is used and conserved at your school? In your Journal, write a paragraph telling what you learned about water use during the school tour.

Home

In your Journal, set up a chart like the one on Activity Sheet 6. Use the chart to investigate and record details about your home water system.

Your teacher will give you a two-part activity sheet like the one below to use with this lesson.

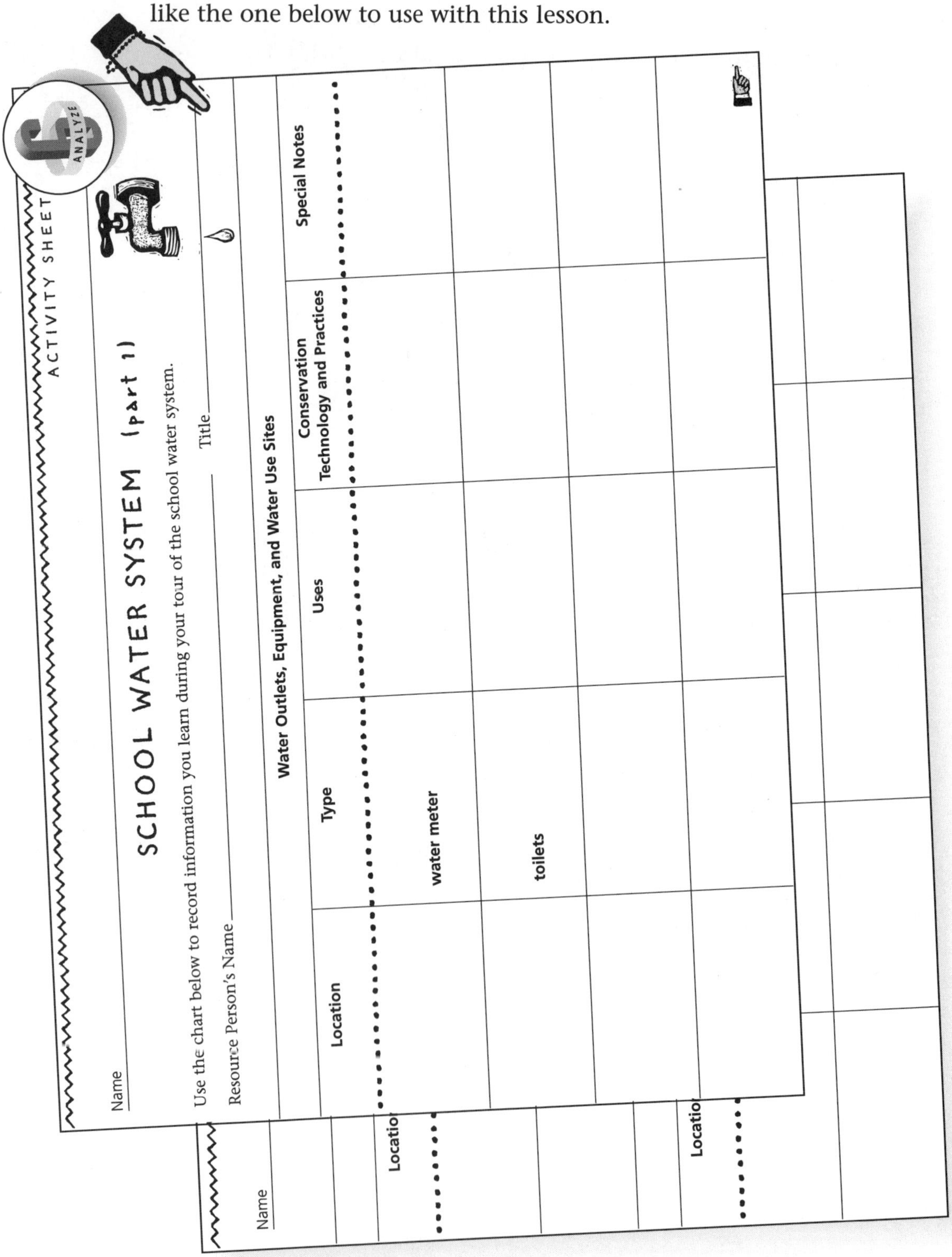

SCHOOL WATER SYSTEM (part 1)

ACTIVITY SHEET

Name _____

Use the chart below to record information you learn during your tour of the school water system.

Resource Person's Name _____ Title _____

Water Outlets, Equipment, and Water Use Sites

Location	Type	Uses	Conservation Technology and Practices	Special Notes
	water meter			
	toilets			

Name _____

Locatio...				
Locatio...				

32 Environmental ACTION Water

PLAN YOUR WATER AUDIT

Plan an audit of water use in your school. Determine the location of water use sites in the school and then organize the sites into research areas. Action Groups will be assembled and assigned to each research area.

Setting the Stage

Discuss these questions:
1. According to your findings in Activity 6, what systems or water use sites in your school use the most water?
2. How will your class conduct an audit of your school's water system?

Focus

A. With your class, plan a strategy for auditing your school water system. Compile a list of all the places in school where water is used. Think about classrooms and science labs, the kitchen and lunchroom, administrative offices, hallways, maintenance areas, sports fields, landscaped grounds, gymnasiums and locker rooms, the pool area, and other water use sites.

B. Organize the water use sites into research areas that can be assigned to Action Groups that will conduct the water audit. You might divide the school water system into areas—first floor, second floor, all outside areas, gym—or you might consider organizing the sites by use—classrooms and hallways, maintenance areas and administrative offices, food service areas, recreation areas.

C. Meet with your Action Group. Use Activity Sheet 7 to record the decisions you make about how your audit will be organized. Find out whether you will need permission to conduct your audit. Are there areas closed to students? Do you need permission to be in certain areas during regular class time?

> **THINK ABOUT IT**
>
> How big are your school grounds? During a good rainstorm, an inch of rain on a half acre amounts to 13,577 gallons of water.
>
> USGS Web site. Water Resources Information, Water-Use Data Q & A: <http://water.usgs.gov>

Analyze: Plan Your Water Audit 33

It's a Wrap

In your Journal, list the school water sites and systems that use the most water. Then discuss with your classmates how well your audit plan has covered these important water use sites.

Home

Review your notes from your interview for Activity 5. Then discuss this activity with your parents and explain your class's plans to audit the school system. Plan with family members how you will conduct a similar audit of water use in your home.

Your teacher will give you a two-part activity sheet like the one below to use with this lesson.

ACTIVITY SHEET

Name

Action Group

WATER AUDIT PLAN (part 1)

Research Area	Action Group (Student Names)	Accessibility / Permission Required	Audit Due Date

Analyze: Plan Your Water Audit

BEGIN YOUR WATER AUDIT

Your Action Group will survey its research area to learn exactly what water outlets there are, decide how best to go about identifying water waste and water conservation, and divide up the responsibilities for the audit.

Setting the Stage

Discuss these questions:
1. Where is water used in your research area? What is it used for?
2. Why is it useful to know how, when, and why people use water?

Focus

A. Working with your Action Group, evaluate your research area by compiling a detailed list of all water outlets (drinking fountains, faucets, showers, toilets, sprinklers) and water use sites (rest rooms, kitchen, locker rooms, science labs) within your research area. You will probably need to visit the area and survey the outlets. Select one member of your group to record your findings.

B. Discuss ways for your group to conduct an accurate audit of the research area. How will you monitor the frequency and length of use of each water outlet or site? One way is by direct observation. Station someone near the outlet for a given period of time to count the number of uses and to time the length of each use.

Consider the best time to audit each site. Should it be done during class time, after school, or before school? Does the time of day affect use? How can you account for changes in use during the day?

> **THINK ABOUT IT**
>
> "It is estimated that it takes 1400 gallons of water to make a meal of a hamburger, french fries, and a soft drink. That's enough to fill a small swimming pool."
>
> — "Water: The Source of Life," from the *1992 The Year of Clean Water Calendar*, America's Clean Water Foundation, 1992, p. 17

36 Environmental ACTION Water

Discuss how you will identify waste or water conservation measures at each outlet or usage site. Are there any leaks? Is water left running unnecessarily? Can people change their habits to reduce water waste? Are faucets fitted with aerators? Refer to Issues and Information section D for material about water waste and conservation technology and practices.

C. Divide up responsibilities among members of your group. Will everyone work together, or will you split up and work individually or in pairs? If you split up, how will you divide up the outlets and usage sites? For example, will one person audit all drinking fountains while another person audits the kitchen sinks and a pair audits the men's and women's rest rooms? Write your plan by working together to complete Activity Sheet 8.

It's a Wrap

On a separate sheet of paper, summarize your group's response to the following question: Why has this activity focused so much attention on where, how, when, and why people use water?

Home

Develop a plan to audit water use in your home. You might make a chart in your Journal like the one on Activity Sheet 8 to record your plan.

Your teacher will give you an activity sheet like the one below to use with this lesson.

ACTIVITY SHEET

Name

Action Group

ACTION GROUP PLAN

Use this chart to record your Action Group's plan for auditing water use in your research area.

Water Site	Numbers and Types of Outlets	Date and Time of Audit	Method of Monitoring Use	Student(s) Responsible for Audit

COMPLETE YOUR WATER AUDIT

Work with your Action Group to complete your audit of water use in your research area. At each site, you will estimate total water use by measuring the amount of normal water flow, monitoring the frequency and duration of use, and calculating water flow resulting from leaks and drips.

Setting the Stage

Discuss these questions:
1. How can auditing water consumption help you identify waste?
2. How much water is lost due to leaks or waste?

Focus

A. Work with your Action Group to develop a method for measuring water consumption at the sites in your water use area. You will need a one-gallon bucket, a measuring cup or beaker that measures ounces, and a stop watch or a watch with a second hand.

You may follow the steps given below to measure the normal water flow for each fixture or site.

Basic Water Measurement Procedure

1. Turn on the water to its normal flow.
2. Start the stop watch and time how long it takes to fill a one-gallon bucket.
3. Stop the timer when the bucket is full.
4. Record how many buckets can be filled in one minute.

Once you have calculated the flow, you will need to determine how long the water runs during each use and the number of

> **THINK ABOUT IT**
>
> If [a leaky water line coming into your house] leaks one gallon of water every ten minutes... you are losing 144 gallons a day, or 52,560 gallons per year.
>
> —USGS Web site, Water Resources Information, Water-Use Data Q & A: <http://water.usgs.gov>

times each day the outlet is used. By multiplying these numbers, you will get the total water consumption per day at the water outlet.

flow rate × length of use × uses per day = daily water consumption

The same procedure can be used to calculate water use at most outlets. It can also be used to measure drips and leaks. You may need to alter the measurement formula to measure very small flow rates (ounces or quarts per hour, for instance).

B. Complete your audit by measuring water flow and monitoring use according to the plan you developed on Activity Sheet 8. Use Activity Sheet 9 to record your findings.

It's a Wrap

Discuss with your Action Group the results obtained from auditing the outlets and water use sites in your research area. Did any of the results surprise you? Did you find any clear indications of waste? Where? How much?

Home

Complete an audit of water use at your home. Create a chart in your Journal like the one on Activity Sheet 9 to record your results. Talk to people in your family. How aware are they of their water use? Record your findings in your Journal.

Your teacher will give you a two-part activity sheet like the one below to use with this lesson.

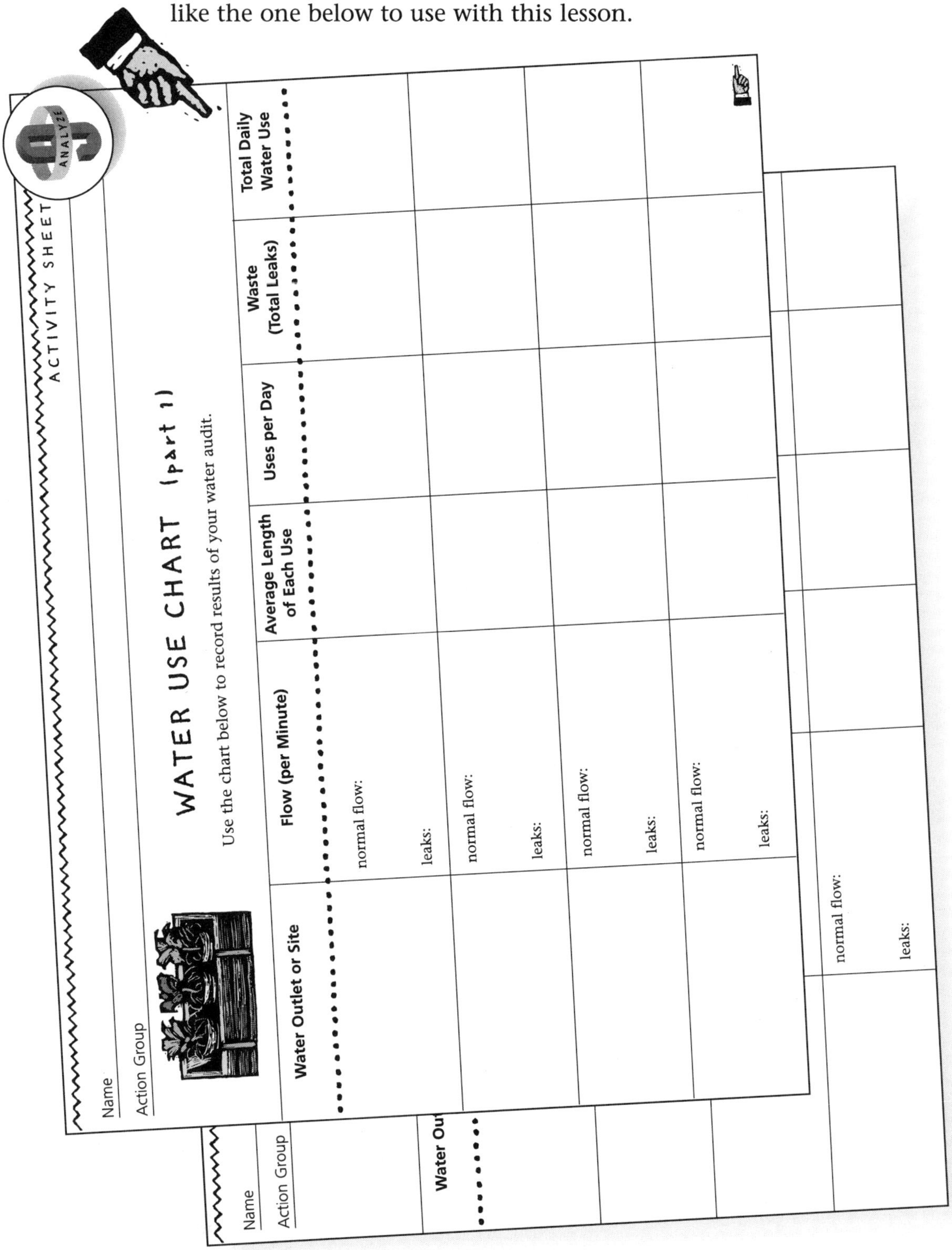

WATER USE CHART (part 1)

Use the chart below to record results of your water audit.

Name
Action Group

Water Outlet or Site	Flow (per Minute)	Average Length of Each Use	Uses per Day	Waste (Total Leaks)	Total Daily Water Use
	normal flow: leaks:				
	normal flow: leaks:				
	normal flow: leaks:				
	normal flow: leaks:				
	normal flow: leaks:				

Analyze: Complete Your Water Audit

READ A WATER METER AND WATER BILL

To get an overview of your school's total water consumption and how much it costs, you will read the school's water meter and analyze the school's water bills. By monitoring the meter twice daily for two weeks, you also will get an idea of water use patterns.

Setting the Stage

Discuss these questions:
1. How much does water cost your school?
2. How does total water consumption change throughout the day?
3. How can a water meter and water bills demonstrate a need to conserve water and also show the results of conservation efforts?

Focus

A. Take turns with your classmates reading the school's water meter for two weeks. Record the reading twice each day: once in the morning and once at the end of the school day. After two weeks, analyze the results. How does water use change during the day and from one day to the next? What patterns of usage can you see?

B. There are two common types of water meters: those with straight-reading meters and those with circular-reading meters. Those with a straight-reading meter are read in the same way mileage is read on an automobile or bicycle odometer. Just read and record the number shown.

Circular-reading meters have six or seven dials. Start with the dial measuring the greatest volume, either 1,000,000 cubic feet or 100,000 cubic feet, and then read

> **THINK ABOUT IT**
>
> "Egypt, whose 55 million people rely almost exclusively on the Nile for drinking water, will have, by conservative estimates, a population of at least 100 million people within 35 years. Yet the Nile will still have no more water than it did when Moses was found in the bulrushes...."
>
> — Senator Al Gore, *Earth in the Balance*, Houghton Mifflin Co., 1992, p. 111

Straight-Reading Meter

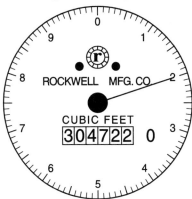

Circular-Reading Meters

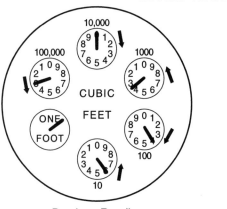

Previous Reading

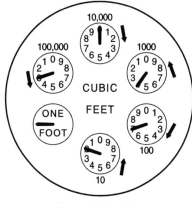

Current Reading

them in descending order. Read the "One Foot" dial as "0." Read and record the number. If the hand on any dial is between two numbers, record the lower number. (The hands on individual dials may rotate either clockwise or counter clockwise.) Read the meters below and write the amount on a separate sheet of paper.

To find how much water has been used, subtract the previous reading from the current reading. Most meters record water in cubic feet (Ccf). To convert your meter reading to gallons, multiply by 7.48. Turn to Issues and Information section E to find more information on reading a water meter.

C. The local water utility company reads your school's water meter periodically and sends a bill for the amount of water used. Complete Activity Sheet 10 to practice reading a water bill. Issues

and Information section E gives additional information on reading a water bill. Then analyze your school's water bill to learn about total water consumption and cost. Compare the most recent water bill to previous bills. How has water consumption changed from year to year or season to season? How has the cost of water changed?

It's a Wrap

Review Activity Sheet 10 with your classmates and discuss how water is used at school throughout the day, how much it costs per day, and how it can be conserved.

Home

Ask your parents to help you locate the water meter for your residence. Read the meter at the same time every day for one week. Record the date, time, and reading in your Journal. If possible, check your family's water bills over the past year to see if there are seasonal differences in water use.

Your teacher will give you an activity sheet like the one below to use with this lesson.

ACTIVITY SHEET 10 ANALYZE

Name _____

 READ A WATER BILL

Below is a typical water bill. Study it and then answer the questions.

Service from 3/21/97 to 5/20/97

METER READINGS

Current	Previous
523,200	511,600

CONSUMPTION INFORMATION

	Units (Ccf)	Gallons	Days	Gallons/Day
	116	86,768	61	1,422
LAST YEAR	124	92,752	62	1,496

Cost per Ccf = $1.04

Please Pay This Amount $120.64

1. Look at the columns under Meter Readings. These figures show water use in hundreds of cubic feet (Ccf).

   What was the most recent reading recorded by the meter reader? _____

2. The service dates indicate the service period covered by this bill. The last date is the day on which the water meter was read.

   When was the meter last read? _____

3. How many months were in this service period? _____

4. The Units column indicates hundreds of cubic feet (Ccf) of water used. Most water utilities measure a unit (1 Ccf) as 748 gallons. The water company has converted the units to gallons by multiplying the units by 748.

   How many units were used during this service period? _____

5. The Gallons/Day column indicates the average number of gallons of water used each day during the service period.

   What formula did the water company use to determine this figure? _____

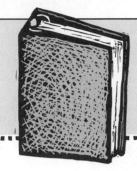

SUMMARIZE FINDINGS

During this activity, you'll review the initial results of your audit and weigh the costs and the benefits of your school's water system. Then you will write a summary of your findings so far.

Setting the Stage

Discuss these questions:
1. How would you assess the efficiency of the current school water system?
2. What is the biggest problem with the current water system?
3. What are the chief causes of the waste you observed?

Focus

A. Meet with the entire class to discuss and combine the information gathered by all of the Action Groups. Include the following in your group's report:
1. consumption for each water use site in your group's research area
2. conservation technology or practices currently in use
3. problems such as leaks, poor usage practices, and other causes of water waste
4. ideas on water conservation
5. any other observations about how, when, or how much water is used

Record information from the class discussion on Activity Sheet 11.

B. Meet with your Action Group to discuss and compare the costs and benefits of your school's current water consumption and conservation measures. Select one member of your group to take notes.

> **THINK ABOUT IT**
>
> "The average American family living in the average American city uses an average of 170 gallons of water a day per person. The highest per person use in the world is in Beverly Hills, California, where each resident accounts for up to 500 gallons a day. By comparison, in Europe that figure is only 25 gallons. And in developing countries, where water is available, the daily average can be as low as five gallons."
>
> — Olga Cossi, *Water Wars*, New York: New Discovery Books/ Macmillan Publishing Co., 1993, p. 28

The group recorder might create a simple two-column chart to organize the notes. One column can be labeled Benefits and the other column Costs. Under Benefits could be listed the advantages of the present way of using water, such as the low cost of water, ample water resources, the simplicity of sticking with the current water use practices, ease of access to water from outlets, current water conservation technology and practices, attractive school landscape. Under Costs could be listed the problems, such as waste, high-water costs, limited water resources, ways the system could be improved, difficulty in changing people's habits, cost of new technology, water shortages.

C. When your group has completed its discussion of the costs and benefits of the current school water system, work together to write a one-page summary of your conclusions. When finished, select someone from your group to present your summary to the rest of the class.

It's a Wrap

Discuss the efficiency of the school water system, where water is wasted, and how water can be conserved. Then write a paragraph telling how your summary addresses those topics.

Home

After you have completed your home water audit, write a summary of what you discovered. Consider such details as how and where most water is used; how water use changes by day, week, and season; where water is wasted; how water is conserved.

Your teacher will give you a two-part activity sheet like the one below to use with this lesson.

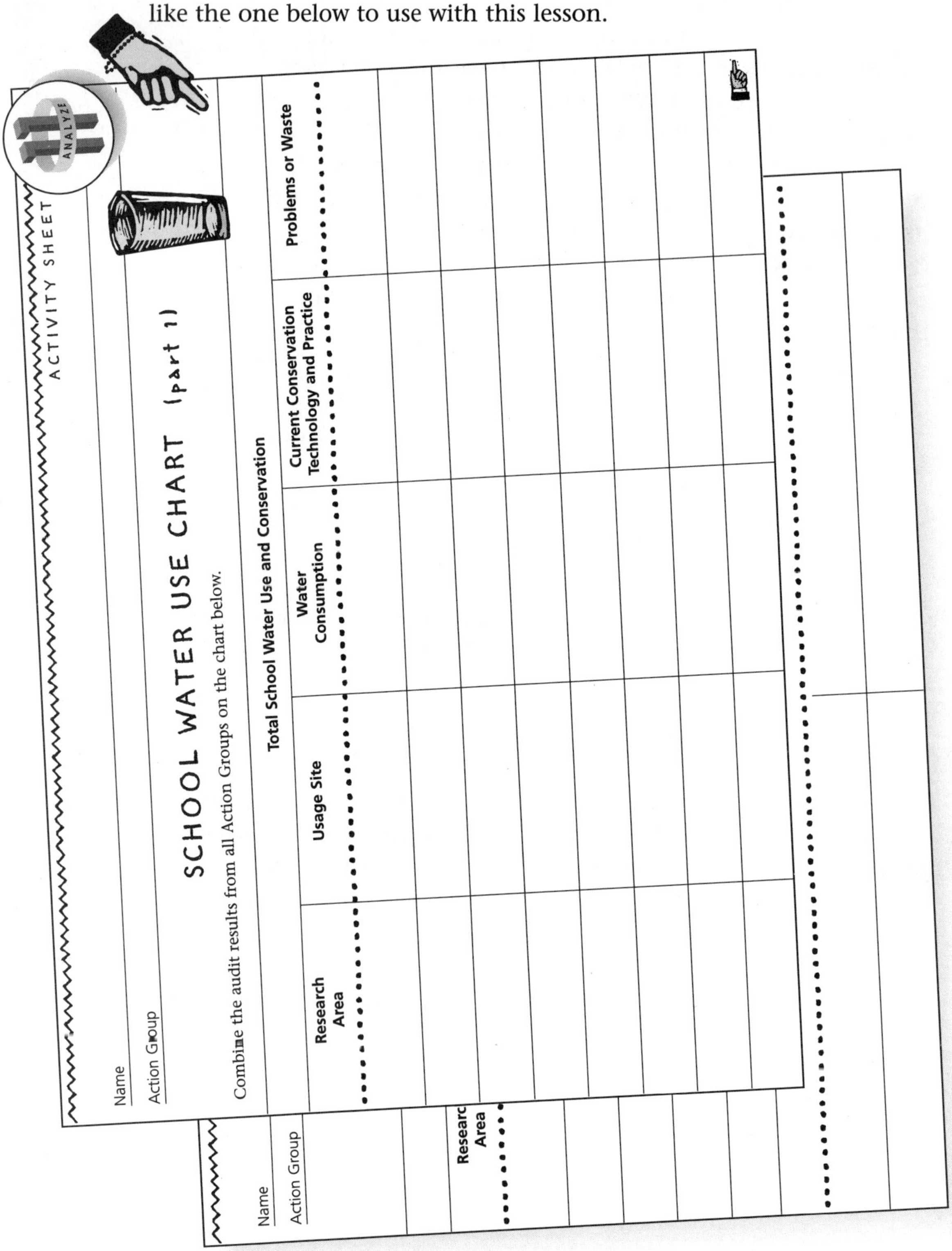

ACTIVITY SHEET

Name _____
Action Group _____

SCHOOL WATER USE CHART (part 1)

Combine the audit results from all Action Groups on the chart below.

Total School Water Use and Conservation

Research Area	Usage Site	Water Consumption	Current Conservation Technology and Practice	Problems or Waste

Name _____
Action Group _____

Research Area

48 Environmental ACTION Water

ACT LOCALLY

You've put a lot of work into your analysis of water use. Now share what you've learned with others in your school and community. With your class, plan a project that will increase conservation awareness and involvement, or use one of the following suggestions.

1. Create water conservation posters. You might design a series of related posters, each highlighting a different conservation technology or change in water use habits that people of your community could use to reduce water waste. Request permission to place the posters in businesses or public facilities in your community.

2. Write a class letter to the editor of your local newspaper about the need for increased water conservation. Urge families, businesses, and government offices to analyze their own use of water and to change their water use habits to better conserve this natural resource. Cite examples from your water analysis as the basis for your suggestions.

3. Organize a school water awareness day. Brainstorm ways that your class can make everyone in school more aware of the importance of water in their daily lives. You might create posters promoting water conservation, set up a display that demonstrates how water is wasted and how it can be conserved, or make a display out of gallon milk jugs representing how much water is wasted each day due to a leak in one faucet.

> **THINK ABOUT IT**
>
> It has been estimated that a typical family of four could save as much as 280 gallons of water per month by installing aerators on kitchen and bathroom sink faucets. Multiply that by every home in America and we would be saving over 250 million gallons of water every day!
>
> — Adapted from *Alternative Energy Sourcebook*, John Schaeffer, ed., Real Goods Trading Corporation, 1992, p. 80

Consider Options

BRAINSTORM WATER CONSERVATION IDEAS

The class will consider ways in which your school's current water system can be improved. After reviewing audit findings and identifying water use problems, each Action Group will take responsibility for certain problems, brainstorm solutions, and investigate the practicality of implementing conservation measures.

Setting the Stage

Discuss these questions:
1. How can knowing the ways in which water is used lead to effective conservation strategies?
2. What kinds of issues should be considered when deciding what conservation measures to implement?

Focus

A. Review the reports and cost-benefit analyses that were completed for Activity 11. Look specifically at the problems associated with the current water system—the water-use practices, equipment, fixtures, maintenance, and other aspects of the system that waste water. On the chalkboard, list each problem. Divide the problems among your Action Groups.

B. Meet with your Action Group and brainstorm solutions to each of the problems you have been assigned. Select a member of your group to take notes. Think about conservation measures that can be taken that will help solve each problem. What are the options? Are there better or more efficient ways of using a water outlet? Can people be persuaded to change their water-use habits in order to reduce water waste? How? Is there some equipment or fixture that can help reduce water

> **THINK ABOUT IT**
>
> "Greek philosophers described water as one of the four elements that made up the earth. To the Kogi Indians of Columbia the three things at the beginning of life are mother, night, and water. The Koyukon Indians of Alaska define cardinal directions not as north or south but as upstream or down."
>
> —Michael Parfit, "Water," *National Geographic*, Special Edition: Water, Nov. 1993, p. 12

usage or waste? For some ideas on how to conserve water, read Issues and Information section D. Use Activity Sheet 12 to write down your ideas for each problem.

C. After your group has finished brainstorming a list of conservation options, go back and briefly evaluate the ideas. Cross out those that are clearly unworkable or impractical. Then complete Activity Sheet 12 by deciding how you will research the remaining options. First think about some sources for information. These might include a visit to the hardware store, contacting the water company, or doing library research. Next, divide up responsibilities among your group members for investigating the options. You may want to work in pairs or individually. During your investigation, consider the following questions:

1. Are any pieces of equipment, new fixtures, or other materials needed to implement the idea? If so, how will they be acquired?
2. How much time is needed to put the plan into action?
3. How much will the plan cost? Think about the cost of equipment, materials, and labor. How will the costs be paid for? Will the plan save enough money to offset the cost?
4. Who will implement the idea? Who will be in charge of maintenance and repair?
5. What are the environmental, health, and economic benefits of this plan?

It's a Wrap

Discuss the following questions with your class: How have you been able to apply your knowledge of the school water system to water conservation ideas? What are some of the central issues you have identified that will help you evaluate ideas for water conservation?

Home

Brainstorm a list of possible ways to conserve water at your home. Then choose the most likely options and investigate them to see whether they are practical and cost effective.

Your teacher will give you an activity sheet like the one below to use with this lesson.

ACTIVITY SHEET 13
CONSIDER OPTIONS

Name

Action Group

BRAINSTORM SOLUTIONS

Use the following chart to help you organize your ideas while brainstorming solutions to each problem.

Problem:

	Options	Research
Changes in Behavior		Who will research? Information sources
Changes in Technology		Who will research? Information sources

Consider Options: Brainstorm Water Conservation Ideas 55

WEIGH THE COSTS AND BENEFITS

You have gathered information about some water conservation ideas. Now you will work with your Action Group to evaluate the costs and benefits of the options you have investigated.

Setting the Stage

Discuss these questions:

1. Can you measure or put a value on nonmonetary costs and benefits, such as those affecting human health or the environment? Explain your answer.
2. Why is it important to consider both long- and short-term effects before implementing a water conservation strategy?

Focus

Report back to your Action Group on the conservation options you have explored. As a group, combine your findings and do a cost-benefit analysis of the options. Select a member of your group to take notes. While doing your analysis, keep in mind that there are often hidden costs or benefits. The following questions can help you analyze costs and benefits:

1. Who will be affected by the change? How?
2. If the option calls for changing people's habits, how will you get them to cooperate? Is this a cost or a benefit?
3. What are the nonmonetary benefits of this option?
4. What are the nonmonetary costs of this option?
5. Are there any long-term costs or benefits?

THINK ABOUT IT

"It is not a revelation to learn that cheap energy makes societies boom, that groundwater in arid regions has negligible recharge, that humans tend to use as much of anything as they can lay hands on. We can ignore these facts and pump, mine, and combust with abandon, or we can recognize these facts and attempt to construct a sustainable society. There will be no painless answers."

—Charles Bowden, *Killing the Hidden Waters*, University of Texas Press, 1977, p. 138

To help you evaluate the options for solving each problem, complete Activity Sheet 13 as a group.

It's a Wrap

With the class, discuss the importance of assessing nonmonetary costs and benefits and summarize how your group has taken them into account in your analysis of the water conservation options. Then discuss the importance of looking at both the long- and the short-term effects of the water conservation options you recommend.

Home

In your Journal, create a chart like the one on Activity Sheet 13 to do a cost-benefit analysis of water conservation ideas for your family.

Your teacher will give you an activity sheet like the one below to use with this lesson.

ACTIVITY SHEET

Name

Action Group

ASSESSING COSTS AND BENEFITS

Use the following chart to help you organize your ideas while brainstorming solutions to each problem.

Problem:

	Costs	Benefits
Option 1	Monetary: Nonmonetary:	Monetary: Nonmonetary:
Option 2	Monetary: Nonmonetary:	Monetary: Nonmonetary:
Option 3	Monetary: Nonmonetary:	Monetary: Nonmonetary:

MAKE CONSERVATION RECOMMENDATIONS

During this activity, your Action Group will give final consideration to all the conservation options you've been exploring. After weighing the costs and benefits of each, you'll select the best ones and develop a finished proposal to present your recommendations to your class.

Setting the Stage

Discuss these questions:
1. How can you decide the best water conservation strategies to implement?
2. Are the lowest-cost options or those that yield the greatest economic savings always the best choices? Why or why not?

Focus

A. Meet with your Action Group and review the cost-benefit analyses that you completed for each problem assigned to your group. Which options do you consider to be the best solutions to each problem?

B. Prepare a convincing presentation of your ideas to give to the rest of your class. Begin by completing the Water Conservation Proposal on Activity Sheet 14 to detail your proposal. You may want to enhance your presentation by adding diagrams, illustrations, tables, charts, graphs, and other graphic materials to demonstrate the advantages of your proposal.

> **THINK ABOUT IT**
>
> "Pilot projects in Pakistan have demonstrated that water losses can easily be cut in half and that the benefits of the water can be raised substantially just by adjusting the timing of irrigation to crop needs, grading the irrigated fields more carefully, and other simple improvements."
>
> —Robert Repetto, *World Enough and Time,* Yale University Press, 1986, p. 58

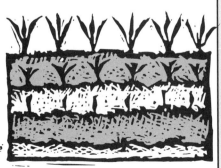

It's a Wrap

 Share with the class how your Action Group evaluated options and considered costs and benefits as options were assessed. Did every group use the same criteria? After the discussion, write a summary in your Journal of your personal responses to the questions posed in Setting the Stage.

Home

Review the cost-benefit analysis you did on conservation options for your home and choose those you will recommend to your family. When you make your choices, consider not only the specific costs and benefits of each option, but think about how your family will respond to each proposal. Will family members be able to follow through on an action? Which proposals are the most likely to succeed?

Your teacher will give you an activity sheet like the one below to use with this lesson.

ACTIVITY SHEET

Name

Action Group

WATER CONSERVATION PROPOSAL

Use the space below to provide specific data about the proposal your group is making to solve a school water-usage problem. You will want to supplement this information with diagrams, graphs, charts, and other graphic organizers to provide a clear demonstration of the benefits of this proposal.

Problem:

Solution:

Implementation of proposal

　Action required:

　Cost:

Long-term maintenance (costs and labor):

Volume of water used at site

　Current system:

　Proposed change:

　Water saved:

Savings in cost of water:

Other benefits:

Consider Options: Make Conservation Recommendations 61

ACT LOCALLY

You have now had the opportunity to explore a wide range of water conservation ideas. Share some of your ideas with your schoolmates and members of your community by carrying out a project such as one of the following.

1. Plan and operate a conservation booth at a community festival or fair. Work with your classmates to create posters, diagrams, demonstrations, and other displays to increase community awareness of the importance of conserving water.

2. Write a series of news articles for your school newspaper. One might describe your class's water audit and what you learned about your school water system. Another might describe your class's experiences with your home water audits. Additional articles might focus on ways to conserve water that can be simply and inexpensively applied in the home.

3. Prepare and teach a lesson on water conservation to a class of younger students.

4. Participate in an Earth Day celebration in your community. Work with an environmental organization to plan and operate a booth or demonstration to increase community awareness of conservation issues.

THINK ABOUT IT

"At the individual level, the collective impact of billions of choices about diet will greatly influence how much water is needed to meet future food demands."

—*State of the World, A WorldWatch Institute Report on Progress Toward a Sustainable Society,* W. W. Norton & Company, 1996, p. 58

Take Action

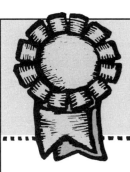

CHOOSE CONSERVATION MEASURES

Your Action Group has chosen the water conservation measures it will recommend to your class and prepared a presentation that demonstrates their benefits. Now you will give the presentation.

Setting the Stage

Discuss these questions:
1. What factors—such as benefits, conditions, or actions—are needed to help put a water conservation idea into action?
2. What factors will help make a water conservation measure successful?
3. How do water conservation measures that you would suggest to your family compare to those you would recommend for your school?

Focus

Each Action Group is going to present its water conservation ideas to the class. Use Activity Sheet 15 to make notes and rate each group's ideas on a scale of 1 to 3. Also jot down any questions you want to discuss further as you decide which ideas are the best. Once all the presentations have been made and evaluated, you and your classmates will discuss the proposals and reach a consensus on which measures to propose to the school committee.

It's a Wrap

Review the information presented, along with your impressions of and opinions about the conservation measures you will propose. Write a paragraph or draw a cartoon illustrating how your conservation measures will succeed.

> **THINK ABOUT IT**
>
> "Whether restoring salmon populations in California, sharing the waters of the Nile River, protecting scarce groundwater in India, or securing livelihoods in the Aral Sea basin, the challenge offers promise—but only if it is engaged in time."
>
> —*State of the World 1996, A WorldWatch Institute Report on Progress Toward a Sustainable Society*, W. W. Norton & Company, 1996, p. 59

Home

Present water conservation ideas to your family. Ask your family to rate each idea according to how much water it will save, how much time or money will be required, how each family member can participate, how comfortable family members are with the idea. Use the rankings as a basis for discussing the ideas. See if you can get your family to reach a consensus about which measures to implement.

Your teacher will give you an activity sheet like the one below to use with this lesson.

ACTIVITY SHEET 15
TAKE ACTION

Name _____

RATING SHEET

Fill in the following rating sheet for each presentation.

Group _____

Plan _____

Costs

Expensive • ————— • ————— • Inexpensive

Health and Environmental Benefits

Low • ————— • ————— • High

Long-Term Effectiveness

Low • ————— • ————— • High

Difficulty of Implementing

Low • ————— • ————— • High

Cooperation Incentives

Low • ————— • ————— • High

Effectiveness of Presentation

Low • ————— • ————— • High

Additional Factors to Consider

_____
_____
_____

Priority

Low • ————— • ————— • High

PREPARE AND PRESENT PROPOSAL

Now that you have explored conservation options and decided on which water conservation plans your class will recommend for the school, use your powers of persuasion to draft a proposal and to present it to your school committee.

Setting the Stage

Discuss these questions:
1. What important water conservation problems were discovered during your water audit?
2. How will the water conservation ideas you are proposing provide both short- and long-term solutions?
3. What were the most important reasons for choosing these water conservation measures?

Focus

Think about these questions as you plan your presentation:
1. What will be the most effective plan for organizing the presentation? Should you begin with the problem, provide the solution, and then outline the costs and savings? Would another order be more persuasive?
2. What is the most important idea you want to emphasize? The importance of conserving water? The savings? The ease and low cost of implementing the idea?
3. How can you use charts, graphs, tables, and diagrams to illustrate and promote your ideas?
4. What tone will be the most persuasive?

Keep these ideas in mind as you and your classmates work together to create an outline. Use the outline on page 69 as a guide.

> **THINK ABOUT IT**
>
> "The struggle for water security will have no winners until societies recognize water's natural limits and begin to bring human numbers and wants into line with them."
>
> —Sandra Postel, "Emerging Water Scarcities," from *The WorldWatch Reader on Global Environmental Issues*, W. W. Norton & Co., 1991, p. 128

I. Title
II. Introduction
III. Recommendation
Include information about cost, benefits, step-by-step implementation, opportunity for participation, need for cooperation, maintenance.
IV. Research and data
Include facts, figures, projections in the form of illustrations, graphs, charts
V. Description of conservation activities already underway.

With your classmates, decide what tasks need to be done and in what order. Then divide up responsibility and prepare the proposal. Use Activity Sheet 16 to keep track of progress.

It's a Wrap

When all the elements of the proposal are complete, carefully review each part and discuss and make any final changes. Be sure that you have included sufficient details to support your main points. Then present your proposal to the school committee.

Home

Write a proposal for the water conservation measures your family has agreed to try. Explain how each family member will participate in setting up and carrying out the ideas.

Your teacher will give you a two-part activity sheet like the one below to use with this lesson.

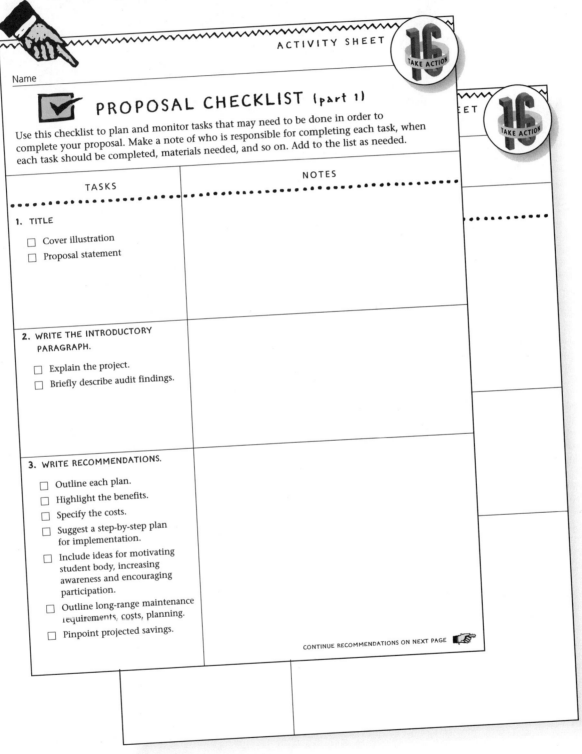

TRACK RESPONSE TO PROPOSAL

You have recommended water conservation measures to your school committee and outlined methods to implement and to maintain them. Now put your efforts into increasing water conservation awareness among the school population and working toward implementing your proposals.

Setting the Stage

Discuss these questions:
1. How can you find out what effect your conservation measures are having?
2. How can you assess the level of water conservation awareness and the amount of participation?

Focus

Discuss the water conservation proposals that you developed and presented to the committee. How can other students and staff in your school be motivated to continue to support water conservation? How can student participation in water conservation be increased? Use Activity Sheet 17 to summarize the results of your proposals and to keep track of progress over time.

It's a Wrap

With your classmates, discuss the success of your conservation plan. What are the most surprising benefits? What would make the plans more effective? In your Journal, write three ideas for increasing conservation awareness.

> **THINK ABOUT IT**
>
> "As the basis of life, water requires an ethic of sharing—both with nature and with each other."
>
> —*State of the World 1996, A World Watch Institute Report on Progress Toward a Sustainable Society*, W. W. Norton & Company, 1996, p. 51

Home

 Write a progress report in your Journal. Think about other conservation measures you can take. Describe the effect your conservation plan is having on your family. How has it increased water conservation awareness? How have the habits of family members changed?

Your teacher will give you a two-part activity sheet like the one below to use with this lesson.

ACTIVITY SHEET

Name

TRACKING SHEET (part 1)

Use this tracking sheet to summarize and monitor the results of your proposal and assess students' conservation awareness.

Proposal Summary

Implementation Report

Month 1 Evidence

Month 2 Evidence

Month 3 Evidence

Savings

Issues and Information

Section A
WATER ON THE EARTH

Water covers more than 70 percent of the earth's surface. Called the "water planet," the earth seems to have a more than abundant supply of this precious resource. There are about 326 million cubic miles (1.4 billion cubic kilometers) of water on Earth. But having enough fresh water, and enough that is not polluted, is a serious concern today.

Water is necessary for all life, and all living things are made mostly of water. A human body is about 65 percent water. An elephant is about 70 percent water; a potato about 80 percent; and a tomato about 95 percent.

Water is a remarkable substance in many ways. First, it exists on Earth in three states. As a liquid, it falls as rain, fills oceans and lakes, and flows in rivers and streams. As a gas—water vapor—it is always present in the air. As a solid—ice—it falls on Earth as snow or hail and is locked in Earth's polar ice caps and other glaciers. Second, it is lighter as a solid than as a liquid, which means that ice floats on the surface of liquid water, allowing plants and animals to live through the winter beneath the surface. And third, water is especially good at dissolving many different substances. For that reason, it is known as "the universal solvent."

Water constantly moves and changes form, but the amount on Earth never increases or decreases. The water on Earth today is the same water, and the same amount of water, that has been on Earth since the planet was formed. Consider the last drink of water you took: it could once have watered the crops in Ancient Egypt, or it could have been drinking water for a dinosaur.

The Water Cycle

The water on Earth travels in a continuous cycle, called the *water cycle*, between the oceans, the air, and the land. The sun's energy provides the fuel for the water cycle. It causes water from lakes, land, and oceans to turn to water vapor in a process called *evaporation*. Through their leaves, plants return large amounts of water to the air as water vapor in a process called *transpiration;* one large tree can transpire up to

470 gallons of water in a day. When they breathe, animals return water to the air as water vapor in a process called *respiration*.

Water vapor rises in the air and cools, becoming liquid droplets that form a cloud. The droplets fall to Earth as precipitation. Rain, hail, snow, and sleet are all forms of precipitation. Most precipitation falls into the oceans. Some precipitation evaporates immediately back into water vapor. Some runs off the land into streams and rivers. And some seeps down through the soil to become part of the water beneath the surface of the earth. Underground water slowly returns to the surface in the rivers and the seas. All the surface water eventually evaporates into water vapor and the cycle continues.

This diagram shows how water moves through the water cycle.

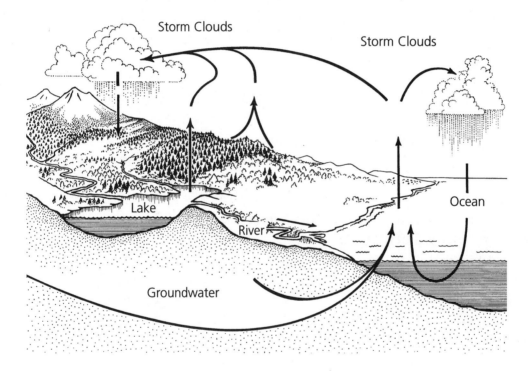

The Limited Supply of Fresh Water

Although there is an enormous amount of water on Earth, very little fresh, unsalty water is available for people to use. About 97 percent of Earth's water is salt water in the oceans. Of the 3 percent of water that is fresh, three-fourths is frozen in glaciers and polar ice caps. Only about 0.6 percent of all water on Earth is fresh, liquid water. And 98 percent of this fresh, liquid water is underground or in the soil.

Only about .012 percent of all water on Earth is fresh surface water in rivers, lakes, and streams.

People draw fresh water from these limited supplies of underground water and surface water. There is a huge supply of water underground, but in some places it is too hard or too expensive to dig through the ground or rock to reach it. The supplies of both underground and surface water are further limited because in many places they have become polluted.

The amount of fresh water that is available is different from place to place and from time to time. Rainfall patterns give us an idea of the unequal distribution of fresh water around the world. On parts of the Hawaiian island of Kauai, rainfall is more than 470 inches per year, while in Arica, Chile, the average rainfall is .03 inch per year. The U.S. receives a plentiful amount of rain—30 inches per year on average—but it is very unevenly distributed. In parts of the Northwest, over 100 inches of rain fall during an average each year; in Arizona and Nevada deserts, rainfall averages less than 10 inches each year. Furthermore, some places may receive no rain for years and then be hit with

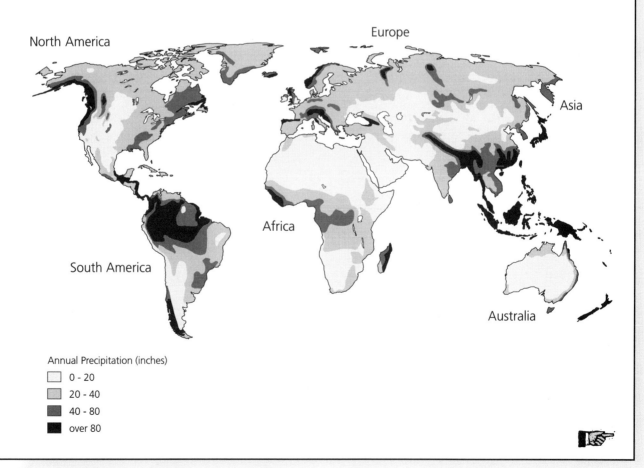

Annual Precipitation (inches)
- ☐ 0 - 20
- ☐ 20 - 40
- ■ 40 - 80
- ■ over 80

thunderstorms that bring 20 inches in a few weeks. The map on page 79 shows the uneven distribution of precipitation around the globe.

Groundwater

About 95 percent of the earth's fresh water lies underground. This underground water, called *groundwater,* is held in the spaces between soil and rock particles. Groundwater moves slowly through the soil and rock—from several feet per day to a few inches per year—until it reaches the ocean, surfaces in a spring or river, or is withdrawn in a well. It is replenished very slowly by water that seeps down from the earth's surface. Geologists estimate the amount of U.S. groundwater to be at least 33,000 trillion gallons.

Areas of rock and soil that store large amounts of groundwater are called *aquifers*. Aquifers vary from a few feet in thickness to several hundred feet and from very small in size to over hundreds of square miles. Some aquifers are near the surface; some are hundreds of feet down. The Ogallala Aquifer in the central United States is one of the world's largest aquifers. It is over 400 feet thick and covers over 170,000 square miles, stretching from South Dakota to the Texas panhandle.

Because it has been filtered and purified by seeping through soil and rocks, groundwater is a valuable source of fresh, clean water. It supplies about half the population of the U.S. with their fresh water supply. Three-fourths of U.S. cities draw water from groundwater sources, and over 95 percent of people in rural areas depend on groundwater for water in their homes. Agriculture is the biggest user of groundwater. Over 65 percent of the groundwater withdrawn in the U.S.—60 billion gallons per day—is for irrigation.

Groundwater is a precious resource that is seriously threatened today, both by overpumping and by pollution. In the U.S., billions more gallons of groundwater are withdrawn each day than can be replenished by nature. In addition to using up the supply, many other problems result from withdrawing too much groundwater. In some areas, withdrawing the groundwater is lowering the land elevation (about 30 feet in parts of California), which in turn causes flooding or alters the soil so that it can no longer support agriculture. In coastal areas, sea water seeps into aquifers that are depleted of fresh water. In recent years, people have recognized the problems of using up the groundwater supplies and are using new technologies to decrease the demand for water.

Pollution has invaded groundwater in every state in the U.S. It enters through wells, through the soil, and through polluted surface water. Once groundwater is polluted, it is very difficult and expensive to clean up because of its slow movement, the difficulty in reaching it, and its slow replacement by nature.

Watersheds

Watersheds are critical to the supply of fresh water and the health of our planet. They are the lands that slope down to a river, lake, or stream. As water runs down the surface of the land, the soil and plants of watersheds collect large amounts of water and release it slowly to the riverbed or lake below. This process prevents flooding and makes more fresh water available by slowing its flow to the ocean and allowing it to seep down underground. When watershed lands are stripped of vegetation or replaced with concrete or houses, the watersheds can no longer function to prevent floods and replenish the fresh water supply.

Wetlands

Wetlands, like watersheds, are essential to our supply of fresh water and the health of the environment. Wetlands are wet places between water and land such as marshes, estuaries, lakeshores, swamps, bogs, and riverbeds. Not many years ago, wetlands were viewed as "wastelands," places for dumping garbage, paving over for development, draining for agriculture, or changing into concrete water channels for flood control.

Now we know that wetlands are an important part of the water cycle. They slow down and store waters, preventing serious floods and making shorelines stable. They filter and purify water as it seeps underground, replenishing groundwater supplies. Some wetlands can even filter out toxic chemicals, pesticides, and heavy metals. They produce oxygen and convert nitrogen for plants and animals to use. Because of the abundance of water, sunlight, and nutrients in wetlands, they are also among the world's most important wildlife habitats.

Wetlands in the U.S. are threatened by development and by pollution. In colonial times there were about 220 million acres of wetlands in what are now the lower 48 U.S. states. Less than half of those acres remain. Close to one-third of the endangered and threatened plant and animal species in the U.S. occupy wetlands.

Section B

USES OF WATER

We use water for almost everything we do. We use it to generate electricity, to make paper and gasoline, to grow our food, to wash our faces, and to irrigate our lawns. We cannot live longer than about a week without water to drink. In the U.S., we pay an average of $1.30 for 1000 gallons of water. One penny buys about 160 eight-ounce glasses of water. We are used to thinking of water as being cheap and endlessly available. Even in desert cities, water comes out of the tap. On average, we each use more than 100 gallons of water a day in our homes. But in order to have water to use, we have turned raging rivers into salty trickles, filled enormous valleys with reservoirs, and drained so much groundwater that the earth's surface has sunk many feet in some places. The worldwide demand for water has tripled since 1950. We all need to make wise use of this valuable resource.

Water Development

To provide more water for human use and to try to control flooding, people have built dams, altered the paths of rivers, and built concrete channels for streams. Over 75,000 dams have been built in the U.S. Less than 10 percent of river miles in the continental U.S. still flow free of dams or other alterations. Water development improves the standard of living by increasing the water supply, providing electricity, and opening waterways for navigation. However, the effects on the environment can be devastating.

In the U.S., much of the land that supported trees, wildlife, and precious scenery are underwater. Serious flooding has occurred where wetlands and watersheds once slowed the flow of water. Rivers and wetlands once rich with nutrients and aquatic life have become unnaturally clean or even dry. And many plant and animal species dependent on waterways are threatened with extinction. The altering of the rivers and streams in the Pacific Northwest, for example, has decreased by 70 percent one of the world's greatest populations of salmon.

People are recognizing the environmental problems caused by altering the waterways and are searching for new solutions. The Army Corps of Engineers, for instance, once straightened the twisting

Kissimmee River in Florida; they are now undoing their work in an effort to revive the wildlife populations, increase the fresh water supply, and let nature do its more effective job of controlling floods.

Agriculture

Agriculture is the biggest user of water in the U.S. Although many crops are grown where rainfall provides the water, irrigation has made it possible to grow crops on land that was once arid. About 40 percent of U.S. water use (from surface or groundwater sources) is for irrigation (over 90 percent in some Western states); that amounts to about 140 billion gallons of water each day. Most irrigation is in the dry Western states, where over 70 percent of irrigation is used to grow crops used to feed livestock, such as alfalfa, corn, sorghum, and wheat. Many irrigation systems lose large quantities of water to evaporation and runoff or result in too many salts building up in the soil so that crops cannot grow. More water-wise methods of irrigation are beginning to be used today.

Industry

The second largest use of water in the U.S. is for industry. More water is used to produce power than for any other purpose in the U.S., but almost all of it is returned to or never removed from its source. Electricity is produced in power plants by turning water into steam using heat from fossil or nuclear fuels or by using the energy of waterfalls or falling water from dams. Many other industries use huge amounts of water—about 36 billion gallons of water each day in the U.S. Water is used to manufacture paper and plastics, to cool hot steel in steel mills, as an ingredient in drinks and foods, and to clean and air-condition factories. Because of droughts and government regulations in place since 1950, industry has improved its water use through recycling and conservation, but water-saving technologies available need to be even more widely used.

Households

People in the U.S. and Canada use far more water in households than many other countries. Our flush toilets, kitchen faucets, lawn sprinklers, and bath tubs are considered luxuries in many parts of the world.

A typical North American family of four uses about 240 gallons of water per day in their home, not including outdoor uses such as watering plants or washing cars. (Refer to Issues and Information section D for details on how much water we use for different household purposes.) People in the U.S., especially in areas where there have been droughts, have found ways to reduce their use of water. These conservation efforts along with new building regulations since 1985 have decreased the amount of water we use in our homes; with continued efforts, we can reduce our use even more.

Environment

People are recognizing that destroying wetlands, damming and diverting rivers, and draining lakes and underground sources to get water has greatly harmed plant and animal life. Aquatic life may be the most endangered on the planet. Some states are reacting to this problem and now have laws protecting fish and wildlife habitats. One of the important challenges today is to figure out how we can share water among households, industry, agriculture, and recreation and protect the water needed for a healthy environment for wildlife as well.

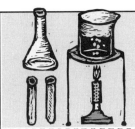

Section C
WATER POLLUTION AND TREATMENT

Water around the globe is being polluted by contaminants such as pesticides, fertilizers, bacteria, oil, household chemicals, and industrial wastes. The Environmental Protection Agency considers toxic pollution in drinking water one of the greatest environmental hazards in the U.S. They have found over 700 different pollutants in American drinking water. Some of these pollutants are known to cause stomach disorders, liver and kidney diseases, cancer, or birth defects. Although it costs hundreds of times more than tap water, many people in the U.S. now buy bottled water to avoid the pollutants in drinking water.

Point and Nonpoint Sources of Pollution

The sources of water pollution are divided into two big categories: point sources and nonpoint sources. Point sources are those that can be easily identified and managed, such as city sewage treatment plants and industrial facilities. The U.S. water pollution clean-up that began with the Clean Water Act of 1974 focused on point sources, and great improvements have been made in reducing water pollution from those sources. However, much of our water pollution is from nonpoint sources. Nonpoint sources are spread out—there is no one point from which the pollutants are emitted. Instead, the pollutants run off the ground or pavement, seep through the soil, or are carried by the air until they reach surface waters or groundwater.

There are hundreds of different nonpoint sources of water pollution. Some of the nonpoint sources are

- runoff from streets and yards
- leaking from landfills, hazardous dumps, septic tanks, and underground storage tanks
- erosion from deforestation and construction
- metals and erosion from mining operations
- overflows from city sewers
- ash from burning fuels in homes and factories
- runoff from farms and ranches

Finding solutions to cleaning up pollution from nonpoint sources can be very difficult and expensive.

Agriculture

Agriculture is one of the biggest sources of water pollution. At least one billion pounds of pesticides and herbicides are used annually in the U.S. These poisons, along with chemical fertilizers spread on fields, seep through the soil into groundwater and are carried by rain and irrigation water over the land into streams and rivers. Many of these chemicals are known to cause cancer or are linked to other diseases including epilepsy, heart disorders, and birth defects. Agricultural chemicals cause serious illness not only to humans but also to wildlife habitat and populations. Brown pelicans, bald eagles, and other bird and fish species were severely harmed by the pesticide DDT, for example, which is now banned in the U.S.

Livestock wastes are another agricultural source of water pollution. The waste from cattle, chickens, hogs, and other livestock, especially those raised on feed lots, runs off into streams and pollutes the water with excess nitrates. In addition, some irrigation methods cause a build-up of salts in the top soils, which eventually kills crops and carries excess salt into drinking water sources.

Industry

Although many industries have improved in recent years in the treatment of their wastewater, industrial waste is still a major source of water pollution in the U.S. Chemicals released into water, such as chlorine from clothing and paper industries, dissolve and form life-killing compounds. Logging and construction practices that clear vegetation can result in enormous erosion problems, causing tons of soil to clog streams and rivers. Strip mining, too, leaves huge piles of cleared soil, often containing metal wastes, that wash into waterways and seep into groundwater. The burning of fossil fuels (oil and coal) by industry and by automobiles releases air pollutants that cause rain to become heavy with acids. This acid rain falls on the land and pollutes the waters, destroying forests and killing aquatic life. Another type of pollution from industry is from the water used for cooling. This water, which is hot when it is released from factory sites, harms the aquatic plants and animals in the streams, lakes, oceans, or rivers it enters.

Landfills, Hazardous Waste Dumps, and Gasoline Tanks

Bacteria and toxic chemicals from the garbage in landfills seep through the soil into groundwater. New landfills must have liners to protect groundwater, but too often these liners leak. Some studies estimate that as many as 75 percent of landfills in the U.S. leak contaminants, many of them very toxic and dangerous to people's health. Hazardous waste dumps and underground hazardous waste wells also often leak toxins into surface or groundwater. Many people have suffered health problems from the leaking of hazardous wastes from such sites. Underground gasoline tanks can also leak, spilling petroleum products into the soil and groundwater.

Households and Urban Life

Pollutants get into our water from people's daily activities. Most sewage from homes—including human wastes, washing and laundering water, and garbage—goes through city sewage treatment plants or through septic tanks. These treatment systems remove pollutants from sewage waste, but city plants can overflow (especially if there is a flood) and septic tanks often leak into the ground. About 20 million American homes use septic tanks, so even a small number of leaking tanks creates a large problem. About 10 percent of wastewater in the U.S. is released untreated into oceans and waterways. Wastewater pollutants are mainly bacteria from human waste, nutrients from garbage and detergents, and toxic household chemicals.

Lead is another dangerous household water pollutant. It enters drinking water from lead pipes in older homes and can get into the general water supply through household wastewater.

In most areas, water that runs off into storm drains in the street flows untreated directly into streams and rivers. Contaminants in storm drain runoff are a serious urban water pollution problem. These contaminants include animal wastes, pesticides and herbicides from lawns, garden fertilizers, soaps and detergents from washing cars, oil from leaking cars, and other litter and toxic chemicals people carelessly let run off into street drains. Some cities are now providing treatment systems for storm drain waters, and some have started education programs to discourage practices that pollute storm drain waters. Trash carelessly thrown on streets, on land, or in lakes, rivers, and streams also causes water pollution.

In the U.S., almost 10 million tons of salt are used on highways each year to melt winter snow. This salt pollutes both surface and groundwater. In some areas, so much salt has seeped through the soil into groundwater that the water supply is unusable.

Effects of Water Pollution

A murky green or stagnant body of water, thick with algae scum, is one of the visible effects of water pollution. This effect is the result of too many nutrients in the water. These nutrients come from water pollutants such as phosphates from detergents and nitrates from wastewater, fertilizers, and livestock waste. They overfeed algae and some plants, which grow and decay, using up all the oxygen and cutting off the sunlight needed by fish, plants, and other aquatic life.

Water pollution is a threat to the health of all plants and animals. Populations of fish, amphibians, insects, birds, plants, and all types of living things have been damaged by the pollution of the earth's waters.

The effects of water pollution on people are many. It spoils the beautiful waters used for recreation. It destroys the environment for fish, plants, and seafood that are part of our diets. And it causes damage to our health, ranging from minor illnesses to deadly diseases. Below is a list from the Environmental Protection Agency of a few of the pollutants found in some drinking water, their sources, and their effects on our health.

Pollutant	Source	Health Effect
Arsenic	Pesticides; industrial waste	Nervous system and skin disorders
Lead	Piping in older homes	Nervous system and kidney damage; highly toxic to infants and pregnant women

Pollutant	Source	Health Effect
Nitrate	Fertilizers; sewage; feedlots	Highly toxic to infants (blue-baby syndrome)
Selenium	Mining; overconcentration of naturally-occurring due to irrigation	Stomach and intestinal problems
Methoxychlor	Insecticides for fruit trees, vegetables	Nervous system and kidney disorders
2,4-D	Herbicide for weeds in agriculture, forests, pastures, and aquatic environments	Liver and kidney effects
Toxaphene	Insecticide on cotton, corn, grain	Possible cancer
Benzene	Leaking fuel tanks; common solvent in manufacture of chemicals, pesticides, paints, plastics	Cancer
Carbon tetrachloride	Common cleaning agent; industrial waste	Possible cancer
p-Dichlorobenzene	Insecticides, mothballs, air deodorizers	Possible cancer
1,1,1-Trichloroethane	Manufacture of food wrappings, synthetic fibers	Nervous system problems
Trichloroethylene (TCE)	Dry cleaning waste; manufacture of pesticides, paints, waxes and varnishes	Possible cancer

Section D
WATER CONSERVATION TECHNOLOGY AND PRACTICES

Water conservation means making a conscious effort to preserve and restore this valuable resource. Water conservation efforts include using less water and reducing water pollution. There are many promising water conservation success stories already. In fact, water use in the U.S. has declined about 10 percent since 1980. Farmers are using water-efficient sprinklers and drip irrigation. Industries are recycling and reusing water within factories, thereby reducing both water use and pollution. Towns and cities are treating and reusing wastewater to fertilize and irrigate fields.

Individuals have reduced water use, too, encouraged by educational campaigns and increased water prices. In Boston, for example, citizens recognized that a proposed altering of their rivers to obtain more water would cause environmental damage. They campaigned against the changes and convinced the water company to promote conservation instead. Water-saving devices were installed, leaky pipes were fixed, and conservation literature was handed out in schools. In four years, people in the Boston area had cut their water use by 16 percent.

Water Conservation Technology

The following information suggests ways to conserve water by using new technologies.

Faucets. Lavatory and kitchen faucets installed before 1980 commonly use 5 gallons per minute (gpm) or more.
- Install newer faucets with lower flow rates. Some newer lavatory faucets have a flow rate as low as 2 gpm and some kitchen faucets have flow rates as low as 2.5 gpm.
- Install aerators on faucets and reduce water use by 25 to 40 percent. Some water departments even provide these free to their customers.

Shower Heads. Standard shower heads use about 5 to 10 gallons per minute (gpm).
- Replace standard shower heads with low-flow shower heads, which can reduce water use to about 1.5 to 3 gpm.

- Install flow restrictors in existing shower heads to reduce flow and cut water use. Flow restrictors are small metal or plastic disks with a hole in the center that are installed in the shower head. The disk reduces the amount of water going to the shower head. Because it restricts the flow, it also increases the pressure of the water coming from the shower head, so the reduced flow is not really noticed. Some water companies will provide flow restrictors free.
- Install shut-off valves on shower heads. Shut-off valves allow you to turn the shower on, adjust the temperature, and then shut off the water flow without changing the temperature of the water. When taking a shower, turn the valve on to get wet. Then turn off the valve and lather up. Turn the valve back on to rinse.

Toilets. Most toilets installed prior to 1980 use 5 to 8 gallons per flush (gpf).
- Replace older toilets with newer ones which use only 3.5 gallons or even less. In some situations, a new toilet costing about $200 may pay for itself in lower water and sewer bills within three years.
- In toilets with water tanks, put a brick or a plastic jug filled with water in the tank to displace some of the water that would otherwise be used to flush the toilet. This device reduces the amount of water used for each flush.
- Add a device called a water dam to the tank to reduce the amount of water used in toilets.

Lawn and Landscape Watering. Use less water on lawns, landscaping, and gardens.
- Use a moisture meter to determine when and how much to water a lawn and to avoid over watering.
- Add a timer to outdoor watering systems to avoid watering longer than necessary.
- Use a drip irrigation system rather than a sprinkler system to water flowers and bushes. Little water is lost to evaporation because the system doesn't dispense water into the air. Water is fed slowly to the roots of the plants where it does the most good. Drip irrigation is not appropriate for large lawns or athletic fields, however.
- Use a soaker hose rather than a sprinkler to water flower beds and bushes. Like drip irrigation, it reduces evaporation and puts water where it needs to be, near the plant roots.
- Install a gray water irrigation system. Gray water is recycled water that has already been used for showers and laundry, for example.

It can be safely used for many nondrinking purposes, particularly for lawn and garden use. Water from kitchen sinks, toilets, or the sewage system cannot be reused, and usually it is illegal to do so. State and local regulations may govern or restrict the use of gray water systems.

Water Conservation Practices

Even without new technologies, our daily activities can help preserve the earth's supply of water. Here are some tips to help you reduce the amount of water you use and the pollutants you add to water. The numbers in parentheses will give you an idea of how many gallons of water you use the old way compared to the new way with some of these practices.

Conserving Water Indoors

Showers (old way: 25 gallons)	Shorten showers. Consider using a kitchen timer as a reminder. Turn off the water while shampooing or soaping up. (new way: 4)
Baths (old way: 36 gallons)	Put the stopper in the tub when you turn on the water instead of waiting for the water to warm up. up. Fill the tub only one-quarter full. (new way: 8–10)
Dish Washing—by hand (old way: 30 gallons)	Do not run the water continuously. Use dish pans or plug the sink. (new way: 5)
Dish Washing—by machine (old way: 30 gallons)	Load the dishwasher to capacity and use the short cycle. (new way: 7)
Brushing Teeth (old way: 10 gallons.)	Do not leave the water running while you brush. Wet the brush and turn off the tap. Use a glassful of water for rinsing. (new way: 1/2)

Conserving Water Indoors

Drinking Water	Keep a bottle of water in the refrigerator so that you have cold water available rather than running water from the tap until it becomes cool enough to drink. If your old pipes might be lead, do let the water run a few minutes before drinking and don't drink hot water from the tap.
Defrosting	Take frozen foods out of the freezer ahead of time to allow them to defrost from the air temperature rather than placing them under a running faucet to defrost.
Ice Cubes	If ice cubes stick in the tray, let them sit for a minute so that they will thaw slightly rather than putting them under running water.
Garbage Disposal	Garbage disposals use a lot of water. Use the disposal sparingly; accumulate the waste and dispose of it all at once or compost it instead.
Laundry	In many washing machines, a full load of clothes uses the same amount of water as a half-load. Use the machine at capacity by only washing full loads of laundry. Some machines have water-level controls. Use the proper setting for the amount of clothes washed.
Hot Water	Wrap insulation around the hot water pipes so that the water in the pipes stays hot longer and faucets do not have to be run so long to provide hot water.
Pipes and Faucets	Be on the lookout for leaky pipes and faucets. Always turn off faucets when not in use and repair leaks.
Chemicals	Replace hazardous cleaning or other chemicals with environmentally safe products. Avoid using products with phosphates. Don't pour harmful chemicals down drains.
Garbage	Find ways to reduce the garbage you send to landfills: buy products in less packaging, compost kitchen scraps, recycle as much as possible.

Conserving Water Outdoors

Outdoor Cleanup
- Instead of hosing off a driveway, sidewalk, or steps with water, use a broom.
- Don't let chemicals or trash run into storm drains. Don't bury chemicals in the ground.

Car Washing
- When washing the car, do not leave the hose running. Use a cutoff nozzle for easy shut off.
- Use only biodegradable soaps without phosphates.

Lawn and Landscape Care
- Water in the evening, at night, or early in the morning so that less water evaporates.
- When cutting grass, leave grass at least two inches long. Longer grass retains water longer.
- Do not collect and remove grass clippings from the lawn when mowing. The grass clippings serve as a natural mulch that will reduce evaporation and keep the ground and grass roots cooler.
- Add mulch to flower beds and around shrubs and trees. Mulch reduces evaporation from the soil and also helps control weeds.
- Avoid using toxic chemicals or excess fertilizer on lawns and gardens. Educate your family and neighbors about what happens when pesticides, herbicides, and too much fertilizer are used on the ground.
- Choose flowers, bushes, and trees that will flourish in your region on natural rainfall rather than exotic plants that must be intensively watered to survive.
- Replace existing grasses with drought-resistant varieties.
- Replace lawns with low-maintenance landscaping comprised of drought-resistant plants, pathways of stepping stones, gravel, or other landscaping materials.

Protecting the Earth's Waterways
- Clean up trash from streams, river banks, lakes, beaches, roadways.
- Be sure paper goods or other litter do not blow away from boats, cars, or picnic tables.

- If you suspect that a stream or body of water is polluted, report it to your local health department, environmental organization, or the state department of natural resources.

Home Treatments for Water Contamination

The Environmental Protection Agency regulates the contaminants in drinking water, keeping them at levels that are considered safe. However, pollutants do still remain in some drinking water. Your local water company, health department, or environmental group can tell you how to have your water tested and give you information about pollutants in water.

Many people choose to use home water treatment devices to improve their water quality. The common devices include the following.

Water Treatment Devices

Carbon Filter	Absorbs many organic chemicals and radon in charcoal filter. Care must be used to keep the unit fully closed if radon is present. Larger units are more effective than small faucet models.
Distiller	Captures lead and other metals, chemical pollutants, and bacteria by using steam.
Ion Exchange	Removes metal pollutants by using resins that exchange harmless ions for toxic metal ions.
Reverse Osmosis	Removes lead and some other metals, bacteria, some pesticides, and other chemicals by forcing water through a thin membrane.

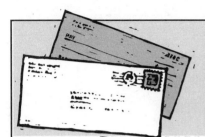

Section E
WATER METERS AND WATER BILLS

Reading a Water Meter

Water meters are located in a variety of places. Often they are in the basement, or they may be in a concrete or metal box buried outside near the curb. An iron lid provides access. Sometimes the lid is labeled "water meter."

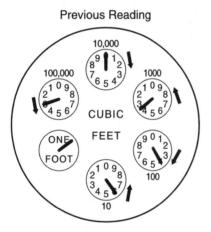

Previous Reading

Read 303,460

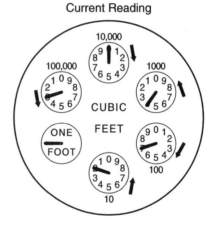

Current Reading

Read 304,720

Most water meters register water use in cubic feet (Ccf). About ten percent of water meters register gallons instead. To convert the gallons to Ccf, divide the total number of gallons by 7.48.

To read the meters, begin with the dial measuring the largest volume, either 1,000,000 or 100,000, and read the dials in descending order. Read each dial counterclockwise, from 1 to 9. Read the 10 and One Foot dials as "0." Most water departments charge for water in units of 100 cubic feet, so the meter reader records the "10" and "One Foot" dials as 0, or disregards them altogether.

The One Foot dial is a test hand used to indicate leaks in the water system. When all water in the system is turned off, look at the One Foot dial. You will find one on both straight-reading and circular reading meters. Monitor it for fifteen minutes. The hand should not move. If it does, there is a leak somewhere in the water system.

Reading a Water Bill

Every water utility company has produced its own water bill, and the specific information provided and how it is organized on the bill will vary. However, the following information and sample will help you interpret a water bill.

Account Number: 0216257-03098
Bill Date: Oct. 17, 1997
Service from 7/11/97 to 10/14/97

METER READINGS		CONSUMPTION INFORMATION			
Current	Previous	Units (Ccf)	Gallons	Days	Gallons/Day
21,634	21,467	167	124,916	96	1,301
	LAST YEAR	174	130,152	90	1,446

Cost per Ccf = $1.04   Please Pay This Amount $173.68

Service from and to date: These dates show the billing or service period, which dates from the day after the last meter reading and runs to the date of the most recent meter reading. Generally, your meter is read on the same date for each billing period. Some water companies bill monthly, others every two months or quarterly. In the sample, the billing period is quarterly, so this bill covers three months.

"Current" and "Previous" readings: In the example, the current reading (21,634 Ccf) was made on October 14. The previous reading (21,467 Ccf) occurred at the close of the previous billing period, or July 10. Note that meter readers ordinarily only read in 100 Ccf units, therefore the dials or digits recording ten and one Ccfs are not reported on the bill.

Units: The number of water units used. Usually this is the number of cubic feet, or Ccfs consumed, and generally, one unit equals one hundred Ccfs or 748 gallons. (One cubic foot is equal to 7.48 gallons, so a unit that is 100 Ccfs is 748 gallons.) To find the total number of gallons used, multiply the units by 748. (In the sample: 167 units × 748 = 124,916 gallons)

Days: This is the actual number of days during the billing period. Billing periods are usually for a regular period of time, such as 30 days, 60 days, or 90 days, but the actual number of days varies slightly because of weekends, holidays, and sick days and vacations taken by the meter reader. In the sample, it is for 96 days.

Gallons/Day: The average number of gallons used each day. Simply divide the total number of gallons (124,916) by the number of days in the service period (96). In the sample, it is 1301 gallons/day.

Section F
MEASURING WATER

The following equivalents will help you take measurements and calculate amounts and flow of water.

Units of Measurement for Measuring Volume

Metric
- 1 liter (L) = 1,000 milliliters (mL) = 1,000 cubic centimeters (cm3)
- 1 milliliter (mL) = 0.001 liter (L)
- 1 milliliter (mL) = 1 cubic centimeter (cm3)

English
- 1 gallon (gal) = 4 quarts (qt)
- 1 quart (qt) = 2 pints (pt)
- 1 pint (pt) = 2 cups (c)

Metric-English
- 1 liter (L) = 0.265 gallon (gal); 1 gallon (gal) = 3.8 liters (L)
- 1 liter (L) = 1.06 quarts (qt)
- 1 liter (L) = 0.0353 cubic foot (ft^3 or Ccf)
- 1 cubic meter (m^3) = 35.3 cubic feet (ft^3)
- 1 cubic kilometer (km^3) = 0.24 cubic mile (mi^3)
- 1 barrel (bbl) = 159 liters (L)
- 1 barrel (bbl) = 42 U.S. gallons (gal)
- 1 cubic foot = 7.48 gallons
- 1 cubic mile = 1.1 million million gallons
- 1 cubic kilometer = 0.9 million million liters

Water Flow

Water flow rates for rivers are usually given in cubic feet per second (cfs) or cubic feet per minute (cfm). Commercial water flow rates are usually given in gallons per minute (gpm).

GLOSSARY

aerator Device that adds air or oxygen to something such as water.

aquifer A natural underground reservoir of water. Gravel and rocks with high porosity can hold large volumes of water. Aquifers underlie many parts of the earth's surface.

biodegradable A term used to describe chemicals, objects, and other materials that will break down naturally in the environment through the action of bacteria and other biological agents.

deforestation The removal of all trees from an area of land. Vast areas of the world have been deforested, principally as a result of the spread of agriculture, disease, urban sprawl, and lumber operations.

drought A long period of very dry weather. Droughts may last for weeks or even years.

evaporation The process by which the liquid form of water is turned into a gas and returns to the atmosphere. Water evaporates from all bodies of water or any wet surface when the air is warmer than the water.

groundwater Water that has been absorbed into the soil and is contained in rock pores, cracks and crevices in rock formations, sand, gravel, and other porous materials. Aquifers are one kind of groundwater. Water from wells or springs are ways of tapping groundwater.

landfill A place where garbage and trash are disposed of by burying under a thin layer of soil.

nonpoint-source pollution A source of pollution in which wastes are not released at one specific, identifiable point but from a number of points or a general area that is difficult to identify and control. Water draining off of city streets and the pesticides and herbicides washed by rainfall from agricultural fields are a kind of nonpoint pollution.

nutrients Substances used by plants and animals for growth.

phosphate A salt of phosphoric acid.

point-source pollution Pollution that is released from a specific, identifiable site, such as a landfill, a smokestack, or the discharge pipe releasing sewage or industrial waste.

pollution Any harmful substances deposited in the air or on water or land. Pollution threatens health the health of people, other animals, and plants, and diminishes the quality of the environment.

precipitation Water vapor that condenses into clouds and falls on the land and water in the form of rain, snow, hail, or sleet. Eighty-five percent of all precipitation falls into the ocean.

respiration The process of breathing, which takes in oxygen from the atmosphere and releases carbon dioxide and water vapor.

runoff The amount of precipitation that falls on a body of land that runs off rather than soaking into the land. Runoff causes erosion and carries fertilizers, pesticides, and other pollutants from the land into streams.

septic system A method of sewage disposal commonly used in suburban and rural areas in which houses are not connected to a municipal sewage system. The system is comprised of an underground septic tank, which holds the raw sewage while it is being broken down naturally by bacteria, and drainage fields where the excess water drains into the surrounding land. The tanks must be periodically pumped out to removed the residue, or sludge, that has not been broken down.

toxic poisonous

transpiration The process by which water vapor and other vapors pass through membrane, such as plant surfaces and skin. Transpiration from plants puts a large amount of water vapor into the world's atmosphere.